THE EXTRAORDINARY LIFE OF

MARY
SEACOLE

First American Edition 2020
Kane Miller, A Division of EDC Publishing

Original edition first published by Penguin Books Ltd, London
Text copyright © Naida Redgrave, 2020
Illustrations copyright © Alleanna Harris, 2020
The author and the illustrator have asserted their moral rights.

For information contact:
Kane Miller, A Division of EDC Publishing
P.O. Box 470663
Tulsa, OK 74147-0663
www.kanemiller.com
www.usbornebooksandmore.com

Library of Congress Control Number: 2020937599

Printed and bound in the United States of America
1 2 3 4 5 6 7 8 9 10
ISBN: 978-1-68464-201-4

THE EXTRAORDINARY LIFE OF

MARY
SEACOLE

Written by Naida Redgrave
Illustrated by Alleanna Harris

Kane Miller
A DIVISION OF EDC PUBLISHING

LONDON

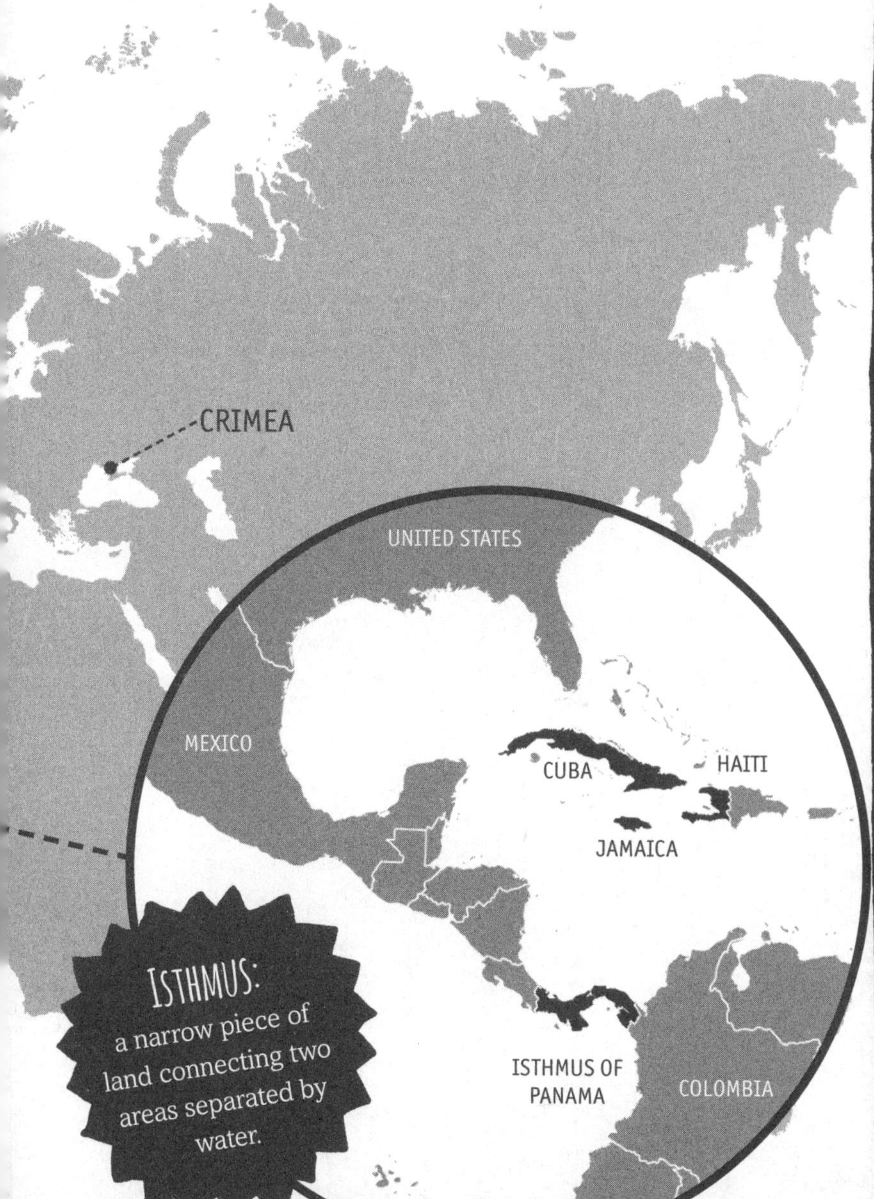

CRIMEA

UNITED STATES

MEXICO

CUBA

HAITI

JAMAICA

ISTHMUS:
a narrow piece of
land connecting two
areas separated by
water.

ISTHMUS OF
PANAMA

COLOMBIA

WHO WAS
Mary Seacole?

Mary Seacole

was a British DOCTRESS and businesswoman born
in Jamaica, who became known as a *hero* for
her work during the Crimean War.

DOCTRESS:
a woman from the
Caribbean islands who
could cure illnesses
with local herbs and
medicines.

On November 23, 1805, Mary Jane Grant was born in Kingston, the **capital of Jamaica**. Her mother was Jamaican and her father was Scottish.

Right from when she was little, Mary learned all about **herbal medicines** from her mother, who ran a BOARDINGHOUSE.

BOARDINGHOUSE: a house (often a family home) where rooms are rented out to lodgers for weeks, months or even years.

Soldiers who were stationed in Jamaica often visited the boardinghouse for *meals and supplies*. They also went to be *treated* for different illnesses by Mary's mother, who was known for being a talented healer. By watching her mother, Mary discovered her own passion for treating sick people, which continued throughout her life.

Mary was a **bold and brave** woman who often traveled alone. This was unusual for a woman during the 1800s, but Mary was very **_independent_**. She wrote all about her travels in the book, _Wonderful Adventures of Mrs. Seacole in Many Lands_. It was the **_first-ever_** AUTOBIOGRAPHY published by a free black woman in the BRITISH EMPIRE.

AUTOBIOGRAPHY: a book that an author writes about their own life (sometimes called a memoir).

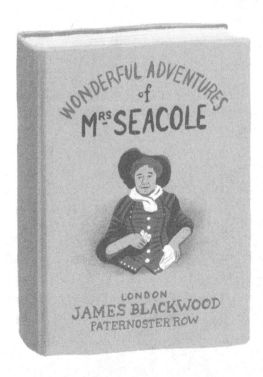

WONDERFUL ADVENTURES of MRS SEACOLE

LONDON
JAMES BLACKWOOD
PATERNOSTER ROW

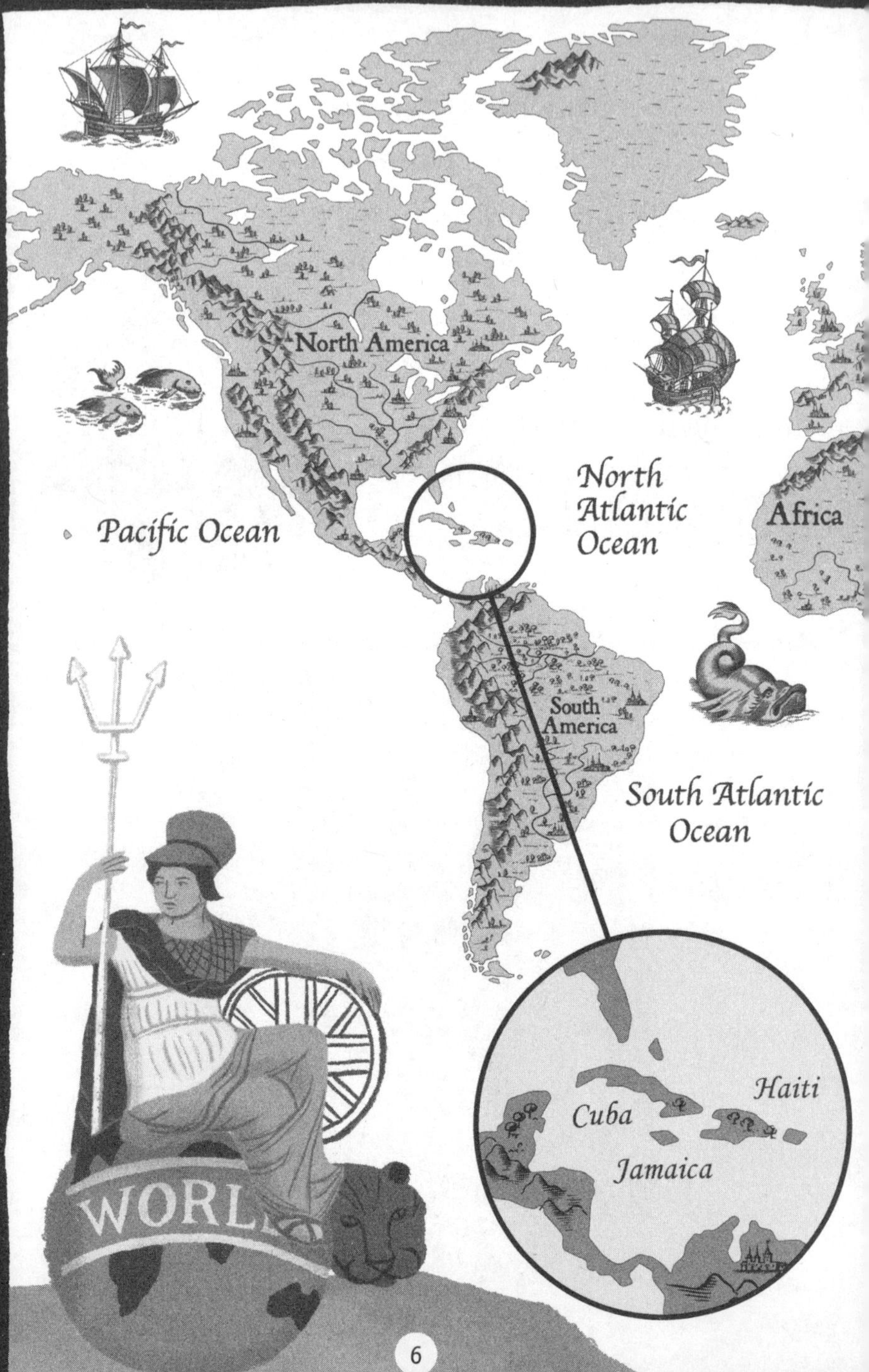

North America

Pacific Ocean

North
Atlantic
Ocean

Africa

South
America

South Atlantic
Ocean

WORLD

Cuba

Haiti

Jamaica

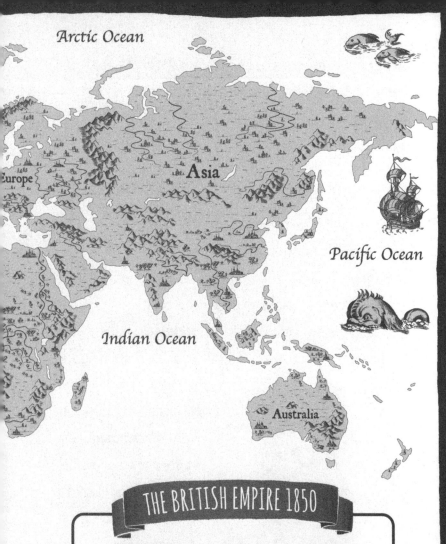

Arctic Ocean

Europe

Asia

Pacific Ocean

Indian Ocean

Australia

THE BRITISH EMPIRE 1850

Great Britain used to rule over many
different places all over the world. It took
control by invading, and forcing the people
already living there to submit to British rule.
This was called the **British Empire**. Jamaica
was seized by the British in 1655.

In her book, Mary wrote about the **difficulties** she faced being a brown-skinned woman traveling overseas because of PREJUDICE against people with dark skin.

PREJUDICE: unfair treatment toward a person or group because of an aspect of their person, like their race, religion or sexual orientation.

At the time, black people were often called cruel names, and many **weren't allowed** to have the same jobs or share the same spaces as white people. Mary experienced this firsthand when she was **turned away** while trying to board a boat with white American passengers. This sometimes made it hard for Mary to follow her dreams, but she was very **determined**. She wanted to help people, and she refused to let anything get in her way.

When the Crimean War had broken out in 1853 Mary had traveled to London to apply for a job as a *hospital nurse* in the Crimea.

Mary arrived in the Crimea with letters from British Army officers whom she had treated in Jamaica that proved she had great *medical skills*. She was turned down by the British War Office, but she *didn't give up*. Instead, she traveled to the war zone with her own money and set up a place where she provided home-cooked meals and supplies to soldiers, and treated them when they were sick and wounded.

Mary is now remembered for her **bravery and medical knowledge** while caring for British soldiers during the Crimean War.

MARY'S BEGINNINGS

*M*ary spent the first few years of her life in *Kingston*, on the island of Jamaica.

Jamaica is part of a group of islands known as the *West Indies*, in the Caribbean Sea. They are found between the United States and South America.

Mary's mother was a doctress and her father, James Grant, was an officer in the British Army.

Mary was always **very proud** of both of her parents, and her mixed heritage. She got her **passion for medicine** from her mother and her **sense of adventure** from her father. Those two qualities set Mary on a path that would see her travel to many different places and touch many people's lives.

At the time of Mary's birth, Jamaica was one of the world's leading exporters of sugar, which was shipped out of Kingston to the rest of the British Empire. Black people were not native to Jamaica; they were brought in by the British from Africa to work as slaves on sugar plantations.

When Mary was young, most Jamaicans worked as **slaves** for their British owners.

However, both Mary and her mother were born *free*. People born free were not owned as slaves, and were able to run their own businesses.

Mary's mother ran a boardinghouse that doubled as a hospital. Here she treated soldiers and their families when they became ill with TROPICAL DISEASES. She was well respected, and the boardinghouse was visited by the most important people in the British Army.

TROPICAL DISEASES: infectious illnesses that appear in hot, humid places.

When Mary was very young, she was taken to live with an old lady and her grandchildren, where she was taught reading, writing and other subjects. Mary still visited her mother often, and **watched in awe** as she mixed herbal medicines and treated patients.

Seeing that her daughter was keen to learn about medicine, Mary's mother started to pass her doctress knowledge down. Mary **practiced at every opportunity**, starting at first with her dolls.

"I BEGAN TO MAKE USE
OF THE LITTLE KNOWLEDGE
I HAD ACQUIRED FROM
watching my mother,
UPON A GREAT SUFFERER —
my doll . . .
WHATEVER DISEASE WAS MOST
PREVALENT IN KINGSTON,
*be sure my poor doll
soon contracted it.*"

In the end,
Mary started to practice
on herself. And by the time
she was twelve, she had become
more involved in helping around her
mother's boardinghouse. She was
learning even more about medicine,
and was sometimes even allowed to help
with real patients. It was then that Mary
decided what she wanted to do with
her life. She would become a
doctress and hotel owner,
just like her mother.

ADVENTURE CALLS

*I*n her early teens, Mary started to **dream of traveling.** She loved to look at a map of the world and **daydream** about her future, using her finger to trace the route a boat would take to England.

In 1821 her dreams came true. Mary **traveled to England** for the first time and stayed for about a year.

LONDON

It was exciting being in this new place that was so different from Kingston, Jamaica. Mary mostly enjoyed it very much, although she was annoyed to meet boys who made fun of her skin color.

When Mary returned to Jamaica, she didn't stay long. Instead, she *came up with a plan*. She gathered large amounts of jams and pickles to sell in England, so that she could stay longer and support herself. With her small business, Mary managed to get by for two more years in England.

This was a big achievement for an unmarried woman at that time. It was unusual for women to travel alone, let alone set up and run businesses.

Mary then returned to Jamaica once again with **even bigger** business ideas.

When Mary got back, she set up a business **selling items** from other countries. To do so, she visited places like Haiti and Cuba, where she bought unique and interesting items to trade in Kingston. Mary's **love of travel** and her **eye for business** were earning her a great living. There was just one thing she missed – she wasn't practicing medicine.

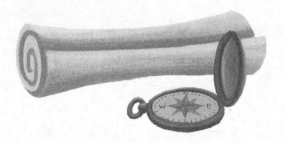

One day, Mary returned to Kingston from overseas to find out that the old woman who had looked after her when she was little was very sick. Mary **rushed to her bedside** and took care of her. Sadly, the woman died in Mary's arms. After this, Mary went to stay with her mother, **determined** to learn more about being a doctress. Her mother welcomed her, and she stayed there at the boardinghouse, learning how to treat patients.

In 1836 Mary married a man called **Edwin Horatio Hamilton Seacole**, a white British merchant.

Edwin was from a naval family in Prittlewell, Essex, England, and was the godson of **Admiral Nelson**.

WHO WAS ADMIRAL NELSON?

Admiral Nelson was a British officer in the Royal Navy, born in September 1758. He was known for his leadership during the Napoleonic Wars. He was killed during his final victory at the Battle of Trafalgar in October 1805. If you ever visit Trafalgar Square in London you can see Nelson's Column, a monument honoring him.

After their wedding, Edwin and Mary *opened up a shop* together. With Mary's business experience, she was able to run it well, and the pair made a good team. Eventually, they shut the shop and returned to Mary's family home, Blundell Hall.

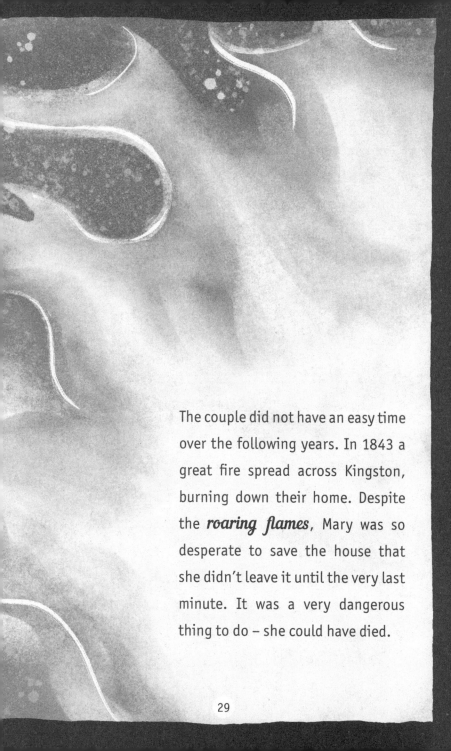

The couple did not have an easy time over the following years. In 1843 a great fire spread across Kingston, burning down their home. Despite the **_roaring flames_**, Mary was so desperate to save the house that she didn't leave it until the very last minute. It was a very dangerous thing to do – she could have died.

Although she couldn't save her home, Mary didn't let this dampen her determination. She set about *rebuilding* Blundell Hall, restocking it with all the items she needed to continue her work as a doctress. In doing so, Mary managed to build a house even better than the one before!

Unfortunately, Edwin was quite a *sickly* man. In her book, Mary writes that she accepted his marriage proposal because she knew that with her medical expertise she would be able to *take care of him*.

In time, Edwin began to grow very ill. Mary decided it would be a good idea for them to move into her mother's house. Sadly in 1844, shortly after moving to Kingston, Edwin died.

"*At last he grew so ill* THAT WE ... RETURNED TO *my mother's house in Kingston.* WITHIN A MONTH OF OUR ARRIVAL *there he died.*"

Losing her husband **affected** Mary deeply. She couldn't move or leave the house for days, and wondered whether she would ever feel happy again. It took her a long time to believe she would ever feel better, but slowly, in time she **began to heal**.

However, **tragedy** soon struck again. After losing her husband, Mary's mother also died. Life became very difficult. As a widow who no longer had her mother, Mary had to earn all her own money to **support herself**.

She tried to stay positive and not to let the bad days get her down too much.

Although life was not always easy, Mary believed that hard work and happiness were more important than making lots of money.

"**Sometimes I was rich one day,** AND POOR THE NEXT. *I never thought* TOO EXCLUSIVELY OF MONEY, BELIEVING RATHER THAT *we were born to be happy.*"

Around this time Mary's **reputation** as a doctress was starting to spread. She would often treat sick officers and their wives.

Mary was also visited by **MILITARY** surgeons, who were very impressed by her medical methods.

MILITARY:
the armed forces;
people who serve
in the army.

In those days, it was unusual for a woman of Mary's age to be unmarried, or "unprotected" as it was sometimes called. After her husband died, Mary had offers from men wishing to marry her, but she *refused*. She chose not to remarry because she was quite happy without a husband.

"IT WAS FROM *my own powers,* AND NOT AT ALL FROM NECESSITY, THAT I REMAINED *an unprotected female.*"

THE PASSAGE to Panama

*I*n 1850 an outbreak of CHOLERA hit Jamaica, making many people very ill. During this outbreak, Mary studied cholera closely. At the time, she had a **military doctor** staying at her house. They used his knowledge along with her medicines, and she **learned a lot** about treating the disease.

CHOLERA: an infectious disease that causes vomiting, cramps and diarrhea.

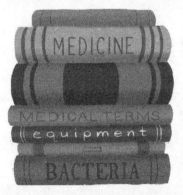

Mary had a half brother called **Edward**, and soon he moved from Kingston to Cruces, on the ISTHMUS OF PANAMA, to open up a hotel and shop. When he moved away, Mary felt an urge to travel. She decided to leave her house to a cousin, and set off from Kingston by boat to help her brother.

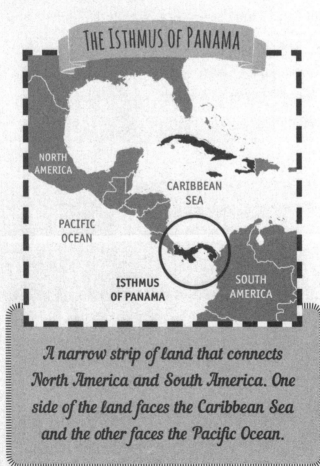

THE ISTHMUS OF PANAMA

NORTH AMERICA

CARIBBEAN SEA

PACIFIC OCEAN

ISTHMUS OF PANAMA

SOUTH AMERICA

A narrow strip of land that connects North America and South America. One side of the land faces the Caribbean Sea and the other faces the Pacific Ocean.

The boat reached the isthmus at a place called *Navy Bay*, which was Mary's first stop. From here she would need to catch a train to Gatun. But the boat arrived late in the night and the next train wasn't until the following morning. Mary described the people in Navy Bay as looking ghostly and pale. They were sick with high fevers and "dropsy," which we now know as

edema. The disease causes sufferers' legs and feet to swell up painfully.

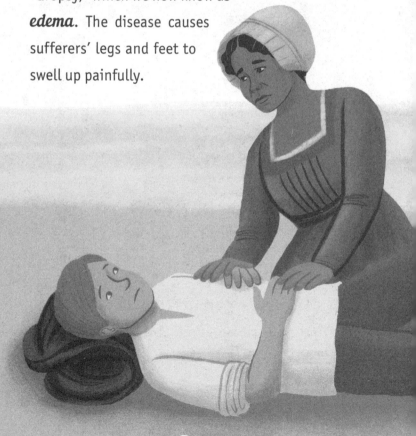

Mary, always wanting to help people, pulled out her medicine chest and did what she could. But she was only there for one night, and what the people **really needed** was something she couldn't give them – decent meals and a warm place to stay.

The next morning it was time to catch the train to *Gatun*. From there, Mary would need to travel by boat again, this time along the *River Chagres*, which would take her to the next stop, Gorgona.

When she arrived in Gatun, Mary was told that small boats could be hired to take people up the river. However, to get to the boats, she would need to climb a *very steep and slippery hill*.

Mary always took *great pride* in her clothes. She loved to wear fancy bonnets, pretty dresses and shawls. On leaving Navy Bay, Mary had put on a light-blue dress that she was very pleased with.

While climbing up the hill to reach the river boats, the thick mud made it hard to keep her balance, and Mary ended up falling over. She was not pleased that her beautiful dress was now ruined! That was bad enough, but things were about to get *even worse* for Mary.

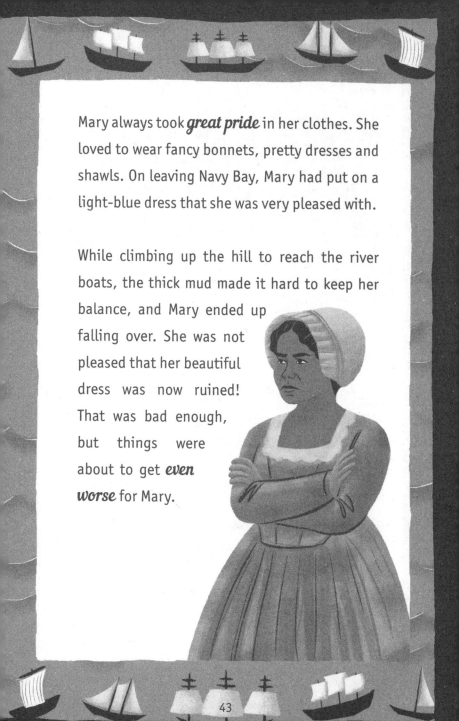

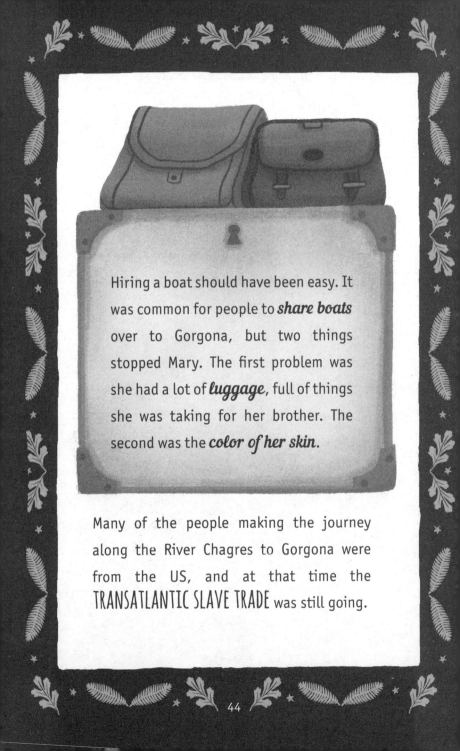

Hiring a boat should have been easy. It was common for people to **share boats** over to Gorgona, but two things stopped Mary. The first problem was she had a lot of *luggage*, full of things she was taking for her brother. The second was the *color of her skin*.

Many of the people making the journey along the River Chagres to Gorgona were from the US, and at that time the TRANSATLANTIC SLAVE TRADE was still going.

THE TRANSATLANTIC SLAVE TRADE

The transatlantic slave trade began at the end of the 1400s. Portuguese and Spanish traders forced African people onto boats headed for American colonies. British sailors joined the trade in the sixteenth century. Many African people died during the voyage due to the horrific conditions on board. Those who survived were treated terribly; they were made to work for no money without any hope of ever returning home.

Because of the slave trade, many people with white skin viewed themselves as better than slaves, who usually had brown or black skin. Some people with white skin did not like to mix with those who had darker skin.

Although Mary was not born a slave, she was still brown-skinned and experienced RACISM. Mary knew she was lucky though, since the captured slaves suffered far worse than she did.

RACISM:
hatred and ill-treatment toward a person because of their race, by a person who wrongly believes that members of one race are better than other races.

At least Mary was a *free woman*. Slaves were the property of their owners, taken from their homes and forced to work under hard conditions. Mary felt awful about the way slaves were treated. She was not afraid to speak her mind about racism, and pointed out how wrong it was in her book.

In the 1850s, 1 British pound was equal to about $4.35.

Fortunately for Mary, she was able to afford the ten pounds it would cost her to hire a *whole boat to herself*. A couple of days later, the boat arrived in Cruces.

Mary's brother, Edward, met her right off the boat. They were so happy to see each other, and Mary was **_relieved_** that the journey was over. Finally, she could start her new life helping Edward run his hotel.

They had to walk a little way to the hotel, and on the way Edward *teased* Mary about how dirty her clothes looked. Although she was usually good-humored, she didn't find this very funny! Her dress was still covered in mud from the slippery hill in Gatun, and it reminded her of just how *long and difficult* the journey had been.

As they neared the hotel, Edward gave her some bad news: there was no bed for Mary to sleep in. *Crowds of people* had arrived from Navy Bay, and the building was packed. But this didn't worry Mary. How bad could it be? At least she would have food and shelter.

Although her brother had tried to warn her, Mary was not prepared for what she found when they arrived. The building was run-down, and it was *crammed full* of visitors.

Suddenly, Mary started to feel quite sad. She had come all this way, only to find there was barely any space for her to sit, let alone wash and change her clothes.

Edward, seeing that she was tired and upset, made a space for Mary in the corner of the bar and gave her something to eat. Mary watched the crowds and the chaos. She had left Jamaica for the adventure of her dreams, but so far it was feeling more like a *nightmare*!

Mary tried to hide herself in her little corner. She now really missed the comfortable home and life she had left behind in Kingston. Perhaps she had made a terrible mistake?

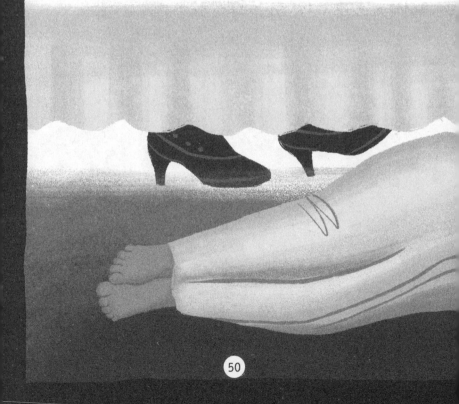

After dinner, the place quieted down and Mary was ready for some sleep. Since there was no bed for her, Mary decided to take matters into her own hands. With a bit of **creativity**, she took the cloth from the dinner table and made a curtain around the legs of a table, creating a little area underneath to sleep in. It wasn't quite the comfort Mary thought she would find in Cruces, but for that night it would do.

The next morning she woke up early, *feeling refreshed*. What a difference a little bit of sleep made! She got right to work and helped prepare breakfast for the guests. Perhaps it wouldn't be so bad after all.

Before long, Mary began to settle into life in Cruces. She even started *dreaming up plans* to open a hotel of her own. For now though, she would stay with Edward and learn as much as she could about this new place.

Mary the doctress

Before long, Mary's skills as a doctress were called upon. One evening, her brother had been having dinner at the hotel with an old friend. Later that night, the friend suddenly became very sick and died. The people of Cruces were shocked by this **mysterious death**. They began to suspect that Edward might have poisoned the man.

Rumors started circulating, and Mary became worried for her brother. She decided to go and look at the body, to see if it would give her any clues as to how he'd died. When she went to look, she recognized **something familiar** about the corpse.

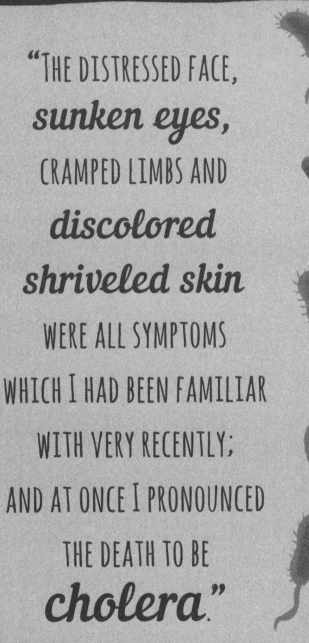

"The distressed face, *sunken eyes,* cramped limbs and *discolored shriveled skin* were all symptoms which I had been familiar with very recently; and at once I pronounced the death to be *cholera*."

Having recently treated patients with cholera back in Jamaica, Mary was aware it could spread, and she knew exactly what she needed to do. With no doctor around in Cruces, Mary got out her *medicine chest* and set to work. She was aware of the warning signs and how quickly people could become very sick. She had to act – fast.

The cholera *spread rapidly*, and many people relied on Mary to treat them. Eventually, a doctor was sent for from Panama. When the doctor arrived, he wasn't familiar with cholera and how to treat it, and became *overwhelmed with the horror* of what it was doing to the people of Cruces. People continued to call upon Mary instead, knowing that she had the experience and medicines to try to help.

Those who could afford it paid Mary for her treatments. Many, however, couldn't afford to pay. She used the money from those who were able to pay to keep her medicines in stock. This way, she was able to also help those without money who needed treatment.

Mary's cholera treatment was a mixture of **natural remedies** that she had been learning about since she was a child. Her mother had long since passed away, but the skills Mary had picked up from her all those years ago were *saving patients now*.

"The simplest remedies
were perhaps the best.
Mustard plasters,
and emetics,
and calomel . . .
When my patients felt thirsty,
I would give them water
in which cinnamon
had been boiled . . ."

Cholera is highly contagious, and after caring for sick people for so long, it was only a ***matter of time*** before Mary herself caught the disease. One day she noticed familiar symptoms in herself. She rushed back to her brother's house and went ***straight to bed.*** By that night more symptoms followed, and she found that she too had caught the dreaded cholera.

Word started to spread that Mary had fallen ill, and people were concerned for her. Lots of people stopped by to ***wish her well*** and bring her gifts. While it was lovely to know so many people cared, she had so many visitors that she barely had a chance to rest for a few minutes before another person knocked on her door!

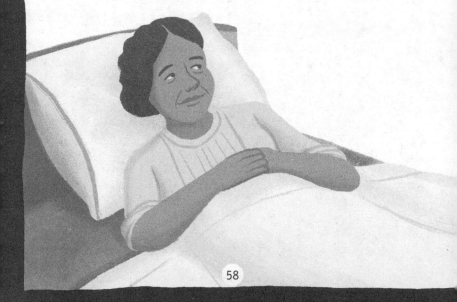

Luckily, Mary's bout of cholera was a **_mild one_**, and although she felt run-down for some time, she was not in serious danger. After a few weeks, the cholera outbreak improved, and the town was able to start living normal life again. By now, Mary had established a **_firm reputation_** as a doctress, and she was often approached when people needed medical help. Mary was happy with this – she loved treating and helping people – but she also decided that she wanted to open up her **_very own hotel_** in Cruces.

The dream hotel

By chance, a little hut came up for rent right opposite her brother's hotel, but it was very **small and shabby**, with only two rooms. Mary gave the matter some thought.

The hut's rent was twenty pounds a month, which was a very reasonable price at the time.

She thought about making it a **restaurant and place to socialize**, rather than somewhere to just stay the night. If she did that, there would be enough room for **fifty** dinner guests. She took it, and within a few days had decorated its dreary walls with colorful fabrics and bows, making the place look **lively and inviting**.

She named it the **British Hotel** and employed a small team of staff to help her run the place. She hired a man named Mac to undertake general duties around the building, and a cook from Cruces to help with preparing meals.

DID YOU KNOW?

Mary also employed an on-site barber to tidy up the men's beards. This helped to attract American visitors!

As a female business owner and single woman, it was sometimes *difficult* for Mary to manage the crowds who visited. *Gambling* was quite popular in Cruces, but it often caused people to disagree with each other and become violent, so Mary banned it from her hotel. She also had to be very careful so that she wasn't *robbed or cheated* – people did try!

One evening, a gentleman settled down to dinner and helped himself to a lot of *hard-boiled eggs*. Eggs were expensive, since chickens were hard to come by in Cruces. Mary and her team would calculate how much money to charge by *counting the eggshells* on each person's plate.

Mary had been watching the man eat lots and lots of eggs. Looking at his plate, however, there were hardly any eggshells on there. Getting suspicious,

Mary sent Mac to take a closer look at what the man was up to. They realized he had been throwing the eggshells on the floor under the table so he didn't have to pay! Mary asked Mac to collect and count the eggshells he'd dropped under the table so that she could present him with the **evidence** of what he'd been doing. He wasn't happy to have been caught, but Mary was pleased he hadn't managed to cheat her.

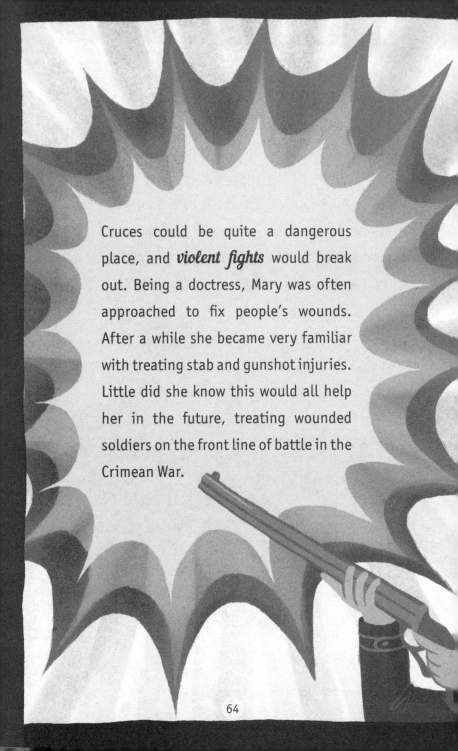

Cruces could be quite a dangerous place, and **_violent fights_** would break out. Being a doctress, Mary was often approached to fix people's wounds. After a while she became very familiar with treating stab and gunshot injuries. Little did she know this would all help her in the future, treating wounded soldiers on the front line of battle in the Crimean War.

A rude goodbye

As time went on, Mary began to want a **change** from her life in Cruces. A friend from Jamaica had suggested Gorgona Island, where he could find her a building for a hundred pounds. It sounded like the perfect opportunity and a great adventure, and in 1852 she prepared to leave.

CRUCES, PANAMA

COLOMBIA

GORGONA ISLAND

In Cruces, Mary had been very popular within the community, so she was invited to many *goodbye parties* by the local store- and hotel keepers. One of these parties was at her brother's hotel, on the *anniversary* of the DECLARATION OF INDEPENDENCE.

THE DECLARATION OF Independence

On July 4, 1776, the thirteen existing colonies were at war with Great Britain. They no longer saw themselves as part of the British Empire, and instead formed a new nation, the United States of America. A group of Americans wrote a letter to King George III, who was on the throne at that time, to present their plans to become free from British rule.

Many Americans were present at the party, and celebrations were in full swing, with everyone enjoying a hearty meal. As the evening drew to a close, **toasts** were made to honor those at the party.

A man stood up and cleared his throat, commanding the attention of the guests. The man thanked Mary for treating them when they had been sick with cholera. She was suddenly in the spotlight.

However, the speech then took a turn that troubled Mary greatly. The man said it was a shame her skin wasn't white, since it would make her more **acceptable**.

When he finished his speech, the guests all applauded. Mary was **furious**, but tried to stay as calm as possible. It was her brother's hotel and she didn't want to give him any trouble. How dare the man UNDERMINE everything she had done, purely because of the color of her skin? Why were people so **prejudiced** against people with dark skin?

UNDERMINE: weaken, make less important.

Mary composed herself, ready to respond. She would be civil, but she would still speak her mind. She was genuinely pleased to have been of help to sick people in Cruces, but she couldn't allow this kind of prejudice in her presence.

Mary said that her skin color made **no difference** to all the work she had done to look after people. She also made it clear that she was **proud** of her skin color, just as she was proud of her ability to help nurse people back to health.

She said that even if her skin had been darker still:

"I SHOULD HAVE BEEN

just as happy and

just as useful,

AND AS MUCH RESPECTED

BY THOSE WHOSE

respect I value."

The guests listened to her speech, though they were a little shocked to see a woman – a dark-skinned woman at that – defending herself to a large group of people.

The time came to leave for Gorgona, and once again Mary found herself building an ESTABLISHMENT from scratch.

ESTABLISHMENT: a business or other organization.

It was not easy, but Mary had the **determination and imagination** to make it happen. With some paid help, soon she once again had a brightly decorated dining room for guests, and this time she had a storeroom and a small private apartment for ladies. This new hotel was going to be mainly a social place for women, as well as for anyone who needed medical help.

Mary had grown tired of Cruces, and she eventually started to feel the same way about Gorgona. **Leaving her hotel** in the care of her brother, Mary decided it was time to return to Kingston.

Parting and prejudice

Mary was eager to **return home** to Jamaica. After saying goodbye to people, she bought a ticket for an **American ship** leaving from Navy Bay and heading to Kingston. An American friend had suggested that she should wait for a British ship, but she was desperate to get back to Kingston and ignored the advice.

When it was time to board the ship, two white American ladies stood in Mary's way. They were not happy to share space with a brown-skinned woman. Mary explained that *she had paid*, and had every right to be on the ship. She continued with her maid and found a seat, trying to *ignore* the women. By now, a large crowd had gathered, none of whom wanted Mary on the ship because she was not white. Some of them became very rude, and called Mary and her maid horrible names.

Mary tried to get help from the *stewardess* of the ship. She asked if she could sit somewhere else, where she would not be in view of the angry passengers. The stewardess did not help and so Mary left the boat.

When she told some American friends what had happened to her, they were horrified but not surprised. The transatlantic slave trade in America had still not been **ABOLISHED** at this point, and there was still lots of racism and violence toward people with dark skin.

ABOLISHED: officially stopped or ended.

Two days after this event, Mary left on a *British ship* called the *Eagle*, and she finally made it back to Kingston.

She arrived just in time – an outbreak of yellow fever was spreading, so she got straight to work helping the sick. She treated officers, their wives and children at her house, and her patients became very fond of her.

One patient, who was a young British surgeon, unfortunately got very sick and Mary took care of him until his final moments, holding him in her arms. The mother of the young man was so grateful to Mary for looking after her son that she sent her a gift all the way from England – a *lock of his hair* for her to remember him by.

In 1853 Mary had been in Jamaica for eight months when she had to return to the Isthmus of Panama to oversee the **plans for her hotel**. She ended up staying for another three months and opened a store in Navy Bay.

While she was there, Mary heard about **gold mines** in Escribanos, a town about seventy miles away from Navy Bay. At the time, companies and members of the public were traveling there to see whether they might have any luck finding some gold. Mary decided to try too, and set off in search of this **valuable treasure**.

There was one occasion where she thought she had struck gold. She put what she'd found into bottles and took them to be looked at by a gold buyer.

The buyer took one look and laughed. Unfortunately the material, which was gold in color and looked just like it, was completely valueless!

Mary traveled between Escribanos and Navy Bay for some time, before making an **_important decision_** that would change the course of her life. She decided to once again travel to England.

The Crimean War Calls

*T*he Crimean War had broken out in October 1853, while Mary had been in Jamaica dealing with the outbreak of yellow fever. In 1854 Mary discovered that many of the soldiers who had visited her hotels in the past had joined the war. She desperately wanted to **help them**. That autumn she arrived in London, ready to offer her skills as a nurse.

The Crimean War

UKRAINE

RUSSIA

ROMANIA

TURKEY

CRIMEA

The Crimean War started between Russia and Turkey. Russia wanted to take over Danube, which we know as Romania today. Danube was controlled by Turkey, so the two countries went to war to fight over who would get it.

Britain and France entered the Crimean War in 1854, to fight against Russia. Britain, France, Turkey and Sardinia joined together and became allies. The Crimean War ended in 1856 when Russia gave in and moved toward peace talks.

Mary had seen in the newspapers that the hospitals in Scutari, Turkey, where the British nurses were based, were overflowing with patients. They needed more nurses and Mary felt she had the experience needed to make a real difference. She had treated all sorts of diseases and ailments. Thanks to her experience in Cruces, she also knew how to treat bullet and knife wounds.

LONDON NEWS

To get to the Crimea as a nurse, Mary had to *apply* through the War Office. She arrived prepared with letters from senior officials whom she had treated in Panama. Mary waited patiently to be seen by the secretary who could put her forward for the job, but the secretary refused to talk to her.

Mary then tried the Quartermaster General's department, who told her to try the *Medical Department*. The Medical Department had already sent nurses over, so Mary was excited – she had a real chance of getting the job. Mary knew that *Florence Nightingale* was already in the Crimea, and her hospital was in need of more nurses. What a perfect opportunity! Mary knew she had the right skills. She hoped that she would finally get to help the troops in the Crimea.

FLORENCE NIGHTINGALE

Florence Nightingale was a nurse who became well-known during the Crimean War. People called her "the lady with the lamp" because she would roam the hospital all night, looking after the wounded. She spent her life improving the standard of healthcare in Britain and beyond.

Mary waited outside for her turn to be **_interviewed_**. She waited and waited. Finally, Mary was told that all the nursing positions had been filled, and that she would not be chosen to fill a vacancy even if there was one.

Mary was devastated and confused. She had **_more than enough experience_**, and she had letters from respected officials to prove it. Why was this happening to her?

Could it be that the British officials were judging her by the color of her skin, just like some of the Americans she had met? She knew she could help the sick. She had been passionate about medicine all her life. Why couldn't other people see that?

"WAS IT POSSIBLE THAT
AMERICAN PREJUDICES
against color
HAD SOME ROOT HERE?
DID THESE LADIES SHRINK
FROM ACCEPTING MY AID
because my blood
flowed beneath
a somewhat duskier skin
than theirs?"

The next morning, Mary woke up more **determined** than ever. She decided that if she really wanted to help, her only option was to travel by herself and **pay her own way** to the Crimea. Once there, she would open a hotel for the sick. Nothing was going to stand in her way!

She left England on a boat called the *Hollander* in January, traveling with her friend and fellow businessperson Thomas Day. They made a plan to open a store and a hotel together. Mary used most of her money to buy the medicines she would need to treat the soldiers. She used the rest for food and clothes from England, to give to soldiers who were homesick and looking for a piece of home.

The lady with the lamp

The journey from **England to the Crimea** was long, and the ship made stops along the way in Gibraltar, Malta and Turkey. Mary would often bump into officers that she knew from Kingston.

LONDON

GIBRALTAR   MALTA   TURKEY

When the boat stopped in Malta, Mary saw some old friends who were **medical officers**. They had just come back from Scutari, where Florence Nightingale's hospital was based. When the officers heard Mary's plans, one of them wrote a letter for her to give to Florence Nightingale. Mary was told to go to the hospital and give her the letter, which would explain that the officers knew Mary and could **recommend her skills**.

The boat continued to Turkey, and when Mary arrived in Scutari with the letter she headed for the hospital.

The hospital was quiet but very full. Mary happened to come across some familiar faces.

One soldier who had been hurt in the TRENCHES sat up in his bed when he saw Mary, and called out to her: *"Mother Seacole!"* She sat with him on his bed, and tried to cheer him up.

TRENCHES:
long narrow ditches that people use for concealment and protection in war.

Mary continued walking around, and although she didn't work there, she couldn't help *lending a hand*. She changed bandages and made the soldiers more comfortable.

Mary stayed at the hospital in Scutari all day, and before she knew it, it was dark. She would need a place to stay for the night. She remembered the letter of recommendation she had, and asked one of the nurses to give it to Florence Nightingale. The nurse had made it clear that there were no jobs available, but Mary thought perhaps Florence Nightingale might allow her to stay and then she could continue her onward journey the next morning.

Before long, *Florence Nightingale* appeared, having read the letter. She soon made arrangements for Mary to stay *overnight*, and the next morning she had breakfast sent to Mary's room.

The next day, Mary left the hospital in Scutari and headed by sea to Balaclava, arriving at a busy port. Her first job was to announce her arrival to soldiers in the Crimea, so she had letters sent to one of the army camps and anyone else she knew that she could think of. Soon she would begin the busy work of **building her hotel** for the soldiers.

LIFE DURING THE WAR

*A*fter a long search, Mary and Thomas Day found an area for their hotel two miles from Balaclava, close to where the soldiers were stationed. It was hard work, but as summer approached the building started **taking shape**. They named it the British Hotel. Very soon it became **well-known** for being a good place for soldiers to visit for medical treatment.

At the British Hotel, as well as getting **treatment** for diseases that Mary was familiar with, the soldiers knew they could also **buy supplies** from the shop and enjoy home-cooked comfort food, such as soup, cakes and jellies.

DID YOU KNOW?

Some soldiers were too ill to make the journey to the hotel. Instead, they wrote letters to Mary requesting medicines, and sent messengers to collect the items for them.

It cost Mary a lot of money to buy the **ingredients** for her medicines, so she charged the patients who were able to afford it. But she never turned **anybody** away. Sometimes the poor patients would arrange to pay her back later. Sometimes they brought her small **gifts**, like apples and other fruits.

A typical day for Mary began with her waking up at around *four o'clock in the morning*. She plucked and prepared chickens for meals later in the day and mixed up medicines ready for treatments.

By *seven o'clock* her first guests would arrive for their morning coffee. At *half past nine*, sick soldiers would arrive for help. Mary treated people until *midday*, when she would leave to visit the nearest hospital and find out who had been *injured in battle* the previous night.

Often she would see soldiers at her hotel for dinner one night, and then **seriously wounded** in the hospital the next day. She made sure to visit them because she wanted to offer some *comfort*, not just for them, but for their families at home.

"I USED TO THINK OF THEIR RELATIVES *at home,* WHO WOULD HAVE GIVEN SO MUCH *to possess my privilege.*"

After this, Mary would return to the British Hotel where the evening guests would gather for dinner. The hotel closed at *eight o'clock* in the evening. After that, Mary would eat her own dinner then get some rest before the next busy day.

As the war went on, Mary became used to the sounds of gunfire coming from the trenches at night, and the *worry* that came as she thought of the poor soldiers in battle. Mary described it as feeling like:

"HAVING A LARGE
FAMILY OF CHILDREN
ill with fever,
AND DREADING TO HEAR
WHICH ONE HAD
*passed away
in the night.*"

During the war Mary also visited the battlefront on her horse.

She took with her sandwiches, drinks, bandages and medicines, ready to help any **soldiers in need**. There was a temporary hospital set up close to the battleground, and Mary helped as best as she could when she visited.

It was a dangerous place to be. All of a sudden shots would be fired and soldiers would scream for everyone to duck to the ground to avoid getting hit. Luckily, the worst injury Mary received on the battlefield was a **dislocated thumb**, which happened when she threw herself onto the ground to avoid gunfire.

Mary didn't treat only British soldiers; she also treated **French** and **Sardinian** soldiers who were Britain's allies in the war.

Mary treated Russian soldiers too, even though they were technically the enemy. Mary had not always been treated well by others, but she believed in treating all people with **equal kindness**.

AFTER THE WAR

*I*n early 1856, news spread in the Crimea that an ARMISTICE had been accepted.

The gunfire stopped and the *war was over*. This was wonderful news for the surviving soldiers and their families back at home, who would see each other very soon.

The end of the war also meant that the British Hotel was no longer needed since there would be no soldiers to treat and feed.

It was difficult for Mary to sell off the supplies and livestock since there was no one around to buy them, so the business that Mary had built so successfully during the war **collapsed** once it was over. As spring came and the troops were bidding Mary good-bye, she couldn't help but feel sad that she didn't really have anywhere to go, and had very little money to build a **new life** for herself.

Mary and Thomas Day were among the last to leave the Crimea after the war. By the time they reached England in August 1856, they had *so little money* that it was impossible for them to set up another shop or hotel. Eventually, they went their separate ways.

Mary found herself not only without money, but quite unwell. Working so hard during the war had *taken its toll*.

However, those who had returned from battle still **remembered** Mary and what she had done for them in the Crimea. She was invited as the guest of honor to a celebratory dinner for the soldiers at Surrey Gardens Music Hall in London. When news traveled that Mary was having financial difficulties, people **donated money** to a fund set up to help her.

In 1857 a *fundraising concert* was held in her honor by the military, and was supported by many high-ranking officers whom Mary had known in the Crimea.

That same year, Mary's autobiography, *Wonderful Adventures of Mrs. Seacole in Many Lands*, was published.

DID YOU KNOW?

Mary had her portrait sculpted in 1859 by Henry Weekes, one of the most successful British sculptors of the time.

Soon she was a household name in England.

Mary continued to treat patients in both London and Jamaica for the rest of her life. She died at her home in Paddington, London, in 1881 from apoplexy, a condition caused by a stroke (an attack that occurs when blood can't reach your brain). She was buried in St. Mary's Catholic Cemetery in Kensal Green, London.

Even though she had been so well loved, after she died and everyone who knew her had died too, she was forgotten about in history for a hundred years.

But in the 1980s her story was rediscovered by historians. Thanks to her book and other records, Mary's **extraordinary life** was reborn, making it possible for generations to come to celebrate and remember her heroism during the Crimean War.

MARY'S LEGACY

*T*oday, there are many tributes to Mary Seacole in both London and Jamaica.

At 14 Soho Square, one of the places where she lived in London, a plaque is fastened on the outside wall.

MARY SEACOLE 1805–1881
Jamaican nurse
HEROINE OF THE CRIMEAN WAR
lived here

There is another similar plaque at 147 George Street in Westminster.

Across Jamaica, at universities and in hospitals, there are many **buildings and departments** that carry her name. In 1991 Mary was awarded the **Jamaican Order of Merit**, which is an award given to a person, living or dead, who has contributed to Jamaican society through extraordinary achievements.

An 1869 painting of Mary Seacole by Albert Challen was discovered accidentally in 2003 by an antiques dealer, who found it hidden underneath a framed print at a flea market in Oxfordshire.

In 2005 the painting went on display at the *National Portrait Gallery*. It now hangs there in the most extensive collection of portraits in the world.

In 2004 Mary was voted number one in a list of the top one-hundred black Britons. The idea for the list came from Patrick Vernon, a British social activist. The year before, the BBC had created a **Top One-Hundred Great Britons list**, which featured no black people at all. Vernon wanted to highlight the many overlooked achievements of black British people. The public voted Mary Seacole as the number one person on the list, which also featured a variety of entertainers, sports personalities, writers, academics, scientists and politicians.

The statue of Mary outside St. Thomas' Hospital in London is believed to be the first in the UK to honor a named black woman. It was built following a twelve-year campaign to raise enough money to create it (500,000 pounds!).

Mary Seacole was a courageous woman who followed her dreams despite the obstacles in her way. She wasn't afraid to *speak out* against the injustices she faced, and she believed in herself even when others didn't. She dared to do things her own way, shaping the *course of events* that we know today as the story of her extraordinary life.

"UNLESS I AM
ALLOWED TO TELL
*the story
of my life*
IN MY OWN WAY,
I CANNOT
TELL IT AT ALL."

TIMELINE

1805

Born in Kingston, Jamaica.

1821

Moves to London for a year.

1836

Marries Edwin Horatio Hamilton Seacole.

1852

Yellow fever outbreak in Jamaica.

1851

Mary opens hotel in Panama; helps soldiers fight cholera.

1850

Cholera outbreak in Jamaica.

1844

Edwin Seacole passes away. Some time after, Mary's mother also passes away.

1854

Returns to London; tries to join war effort as a nurse and is refused.

1855

Travels to the Crimea; meets Florence Nightingale.

1856

Returns to England with no money; guest of honor at celebratory dinner for soldiers.

1860

Travels between England and Jamaica regularly.

1859

Henry Weekes creates sculpture of Mary.

1857

Wonderful Adventures of Mrs. Seacole in Many Lands published.

1869
Albert Charles Challen
paints portrait of Mary.

1870
Returns to
London for good.

1881
Dies; buried in St. Mary's
Catholic Cemetery,
Kensal Green.

2005

Newly discovered Mary Seacole portrait goes on display at the National Portrait Gallery.

2004

Voted first in a poll of the top one-hundred black Britons.

1991

Awarded the Jamaican Order of Merit.

SOME THINGS TO THINK ABOUT

Mary Seacole faced discrimination because of the color of her skin. Racism still exists in our world in many different forms. What do you think Mary Seacole would have to say about it if she was alive today?

Mary wrote her own account of her life in the book, *Wonderful Adventures of Mrs. Seacole in Many Lands*. Some people claim that this isn't a full picture of her life because it's all from her own point of view. How valuable do you think it is to have access to autobiographies – that is, books written by people about their own lives? How important is it to read about a person's experiences in their own words?

Mary Seacole's story was unknown for many years, and Florence Nightingale, who did similar wonderful, lifesaving things, was famous across the world. Why do you think Florence was remembered, while Mary was forgotten?

Index

Quote Sources

All quotes throughout are taken from *Wonderful Adventures of Mrs. Seacole in Many Lands* by Mary Seacole (Cambridge University Press, 2013) except the following:

p. 69: *A History of Britain in 21 Women* (J. Murray, Oneworld Publications, 2016)